# MY FIRST BOOK OF SOCCER

Sports Illustrated KIDS

She said we were going to play football.

He really needs this book.

By Beth Bugler and Mark Bechtel

A ROOKIE Book

Illustrations by Bill Hinds

Soccer, or football as it's known in the rest of the world, is a sport played by

# TWO TEAMS.

The players try to score goals by getting a ball into a net without using their hands. Each team has

on the field at one time.

The game is played in **TWO HALVES** that are **45 MINUTES** long. Unlike in other sports, the clock starts at zero and counts up.

The **REFEREE** is in charge of the game. He keeps track of the time, and gets help from two assistants called **LINESMEN.**

The players line up at different positions.

Dude, where's that five bucks you owe me?

Hey guys, which is the position that runs the least?

**FORWARDS** try to score goals.

**DEFENDERS** try to keep the other team from scoring.

**MIDFIELDERS** try to help score goals AND help keep the other team from scoring.

**HALF 1ST**

The team with the ball is the
**ATTACKING**
team.

The other players are the
**DEFENDING**
team.

She's got the ball and makes a **PASS** to her teammate

who then **DRIBBLES** the ball up the field with her feet.

Look out!
Here comes a defender
who makes a

# TACKLE

and steals away the
ball with his foot.


TIME
5:12

Maybe this will
come in handy
after all.

HALF

1ST

Whoops. A player knocked the ball over the sideline. The other team gets to take a

# THROW-IN

from the spot where the ball went out of play.

HALF
1ST

He's got the goal in sight and takes a

# SHOT.

It's headed toward the net. Will the goalkeeper stop it?

Darn! My aim was so off!

Yes! The goalkeeper makes a

# SAVE!

He used his hands to stop the shot.

Are we doing "Head, shoulders, knees, and toes?"

TIME

21:10

But the ball went over the goal line.
Since the defending team was the last
to touch it, the other team gets a

# CORNER KICK

from the nearest corner flag.

Do you think she has a plan?

I'm sure her plan is to score!

The kick comes in high, so his teammate jumps up and hits a

# HEADER

toward the net.

That's how the pros use their heads!

OAAL!!

# FTIME!!

The clock hits 45 minutes. The ref blows his whistle and the players take a short break.

The game gets ready to start again. But first, the coach decides to make a

# SUBSTITUTION.

A new player comes off the bench and into the game.

Does she have to go home now?

The linesman has his flag up because number 10 was

# OFFSIDE.

That means he was closer to the goal than all of the defensive players when he got the ball. The rule prevents players from just hanging out near the net and scoring easy goals.

TIME
53:30

Is that a quarter in the grass?

Ah! There goes my plan to score!

Look! She tries to make a tackle, but she trips her opponent instead. That's a

# FOUL!

Even I know tripping is wrong!

Since the foul was serious, the referee shows the player a

# YELLOW CARD.

That's a warning that he'd better not do it again.

The attacking team gets a

# FREE KICK.

The attacking team gets to place the ball where the foul happened. They can either pass the ball or take a shot at the goal. The defense sets up a

# WALL.

But it looks like she's going to try to bend the ball around them and into the net!

No way I'm sitting on THAT wall.

Oh, no! A player who already has a yellow card has committed another bad foul. The referee brings out a

# RED CARD

and sends her out of the game.

Buh, bye!

The ball has gone over the goal line, but this time it was kicked out by the attacking team. That means the other side's goalie gets to take a

# GOAL KICK.

She places the ball on the goal box and knocks it all the way down the field.

The clock has almost reached 90 minutes, and the score is tied. Whoa! Did you see that? That defender knocked down the ball with his hand! The ref calls a

# HAND BALL.

And since it happened in the penalty area, the other team gets a . . .

# ...PENALTY KICK.

They get a free shot and only the goalkeeper is allowed to try to stop it.

It goes in!
Her team has
the lead!

Stay back everyone!

PEEP! PEEP! PEEP!

GAME OVER!

And to celebrate—the players exchange jerseys!

Are you a medium? I'm a medium.

Library of Congress Cataloging-in-Publication Data available upon request.

Printed in China
ISBN 978-1-63727-681-5

This book is available in quantity at special discounts for your group or organization. For further information, contact:

Triumph Books LLC
814 North Franklin Street
Chicago, Illinois 60610
(312) 337-0747
www.triumphbooks.com

PHOTO CREDITS, in order: Page 1: AP Photo/Thibault Camus; Pages 2-3: Erick W. Rasco; Page 6: Roy K Miller/ISI Photos/USSF; Page 7: Howard Smith/ISI Photos/USSF (Turner), Erick W. Rasco (referee); Pages 8-9: Erick W. Rasco; Page 10: Simon Bruty; Page 12: Melissa Tamez/Icon Sportswire; Page 13: Brad Smith/ISI Photos/USSF; Page 14: Glyn Kirk/AFP; Page 15: Darren Staples/CSM; Page 16: Lindsey Parnaby/AFP; Page 17: Catherine Ivill/AVP; Page 18: Harriet Lander/Chelsea FC (Reiten), Press Association (players); Pages 20-21: Julian Finney/UEFA; Page 23: Erick W. Rasco; Page 24: Marcelo Endelli/Getty Images (Argentina), Pro Shots/Sipa USA (France); Page 27: Elsa/Getty Images; Page 28: Simon Bruty; Page 29: Lars Ronbog/FrontZoneSport; Page 31: Erick W. Rasco; Page 33: Isabel Infantes/PA Images; Page 34: Robin Alam/Icon Sportswire; Page 36: Ralf Ibing/picture-alliance; Page 37: Darren Staples/Sportimage/CSM; Page 39: Cody Froggatt/News Images/Sipa USA; Page 40: Glyn Kirk/AFP; Page 43: Lindsey Parnaby/AFP; Page 45: Ben Stansall/AFP; Pages 46-47: Erick W. Rasco (referee), Omar Torres/AFP (Bejarano/Messi); Back cover: Cliff Welch/Icon Sportswire.

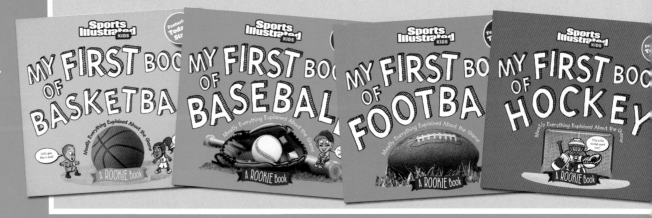